Lerner SPORTS™

GREATEST OF ALL TIME PLAYERS

# G.O.A.T. BASEBALL SHORTSTOPS

Alexander Lowe

Lerner Publications ◆ Minneapolis

Lerner Publications Company
An imprint of Lerner Publishing Group, Inc.
241 First Avenue North
Minneapolis, MN 55401 USA

For reading levels and more information, look up this title at www.lernerbooks.com.

Main body text set in Aptifer Sans LT Pro.
Typeface provided by Linotype AG.

**Library of Congress Cataloging-in-Publication Data**

Names: Lowe, Alexander, author.
Title: G.O.A.T. baseball shortstops / Alexander Lowe.
Other titles: Greatest of all time baseball shortstops
Description: Minneapolis : Lerner Publications, 2022. | Series: Greatest of All Time Players (Lerner Sports) | Includes bibliographical references and index. | Audience: Ages 7–11 | Audience: Grades 4–6 | Summary: “The greatest shortstops of all time played incredible defense, excelled with the bat, and led their teams to championships. Learn about the top shortstops in MLB history and create your own ranking of the best players”— Provided by publisher.
Identifiers: LCCN 2021018556 (print) | LCCN 2021018557 (ebook) | ISBN 9781728441115 (library binding) | ISBN 9781728448435 (paperback) | ISBN 9781728444765 (ebook)
Subjects: LCSH: Baseball players—United States—Biography—Juvenile literature. | Shortstop (Baseball)—Juvenile literature.
Classification: LCC GV865.A1 L68 2022 (print) | LCC GV865.A1 (ebook) | DDC 796.357092/273 [B]—dc23

LC record available at https://lccn.loc.gov/2021018556
LC ebook record available at https://lccn.loc.gov/2021018557

Manufactured in the United States of America
1-49882-49725-7/12/2021

# TABLE OF CONTENTS

Derek Jeter wowed Yankees fans with his batting skills and his athletic throws in the field.

# SWEET SWINGING SHORTSTOPS

The New York Yankees pitcher glances at the Boston Red Sox player on first base and then throws the pitch. The batter hits a ground ball up the middle of the diamond. New York shortstop Derek Jeter dives for the ball. He jumps to his feet and throws it to second base. The second baseman catches the ball and flings it to first. The umpire signals out! Jeter started a game-saving double play.

# FACTS AT A GLANCE

- » **BARRY LARKIN** PLAYED FOR THE CINCINNATI REDS FOR 19 SEASONS.
- » **ERNIE BANKS** WAS THE FIRST PLAYER IN CHICAGO CUBS HISTORY WHOSE JERSEY NUMBER WAS RETIRED BY THE TEAM.
- » **DEREK JETER** IS THE ONLY PLAYER TO WIN THE ALL-STAR GAME MOST VALUABLE PLAYER (MVP) AWARD AND THE WORLD SERIES MVP AWARD IN THE SAME SEASON.
- » **OZZIE SMITH** WAS NICKNAMED THE WIZARD OF OZ.

Major League Baseball (MLB) started in 1903. By that time, people had been playing the sport for over fifty years. The game has changed in many ways since its beginning. One of the biggest changes came in 1947. That year, Jackie Robinson (*right*) became the first Black player to take the field in MLB. Before then, no Black players were allowed to play in the league. Many of the greatest Black players in history never had the opportunity to play in the major leagues.

Shortstops usually play between second and third base. They have to be quick to get to hard-hit balls. Shortstops also need strong arms to throw the ball all the way across the field to first base.

Alex Rodriguez was a skilled shortstop for the Seattle Mariners and the Texas Rangers for 10 seasons before taking over at third base for the Yankees.

Barry Larkin of the Reds was one of the greatest defensive shortstops of all time.

Shortstops are often strong offensive players as well. Some of the best use their speed to score runs. Others are great power hitters. The best shortstops in baseball history have been able to do both.

It can be hard to rank the greatest shortstops. Many great players have played the position. The best shortstops are some of the greatest of all time (G.O.A.T.)!

## No. 10 PEE WEE REESE

Pee Wee Reese was the captain of the Brooklyn Dodgers when they were at their best. The Dodgers won the National League championship seven times with Reese on the team. He also led them to a World Series victory in 1955. The Dodgers were the best team in the National League, and Reese was their heart and soul.

Reese finished in the top 10 in National League MVP voting eight times. He was a ten-time All-Star. He had solid offensive numbers. But his contributions were much bigger than his numbers showed.

Reese was a great defender. He led the league in putouts four times and in double plays twice. His double play partner for much of his career was Jackie Robinson, the first Black player to play in the league.

## PEE WEE REESE STATS

| | |
|---|---|
| Batting Average | .269 |
| Hits | 2,170 |
| Home Runs | 126 |
| RBIs | 885 |

# No. 9 OZZIE SMITH

When it comes to defense, there may have never been a better shortstop than Ozzie Smith. His range seemed to be unlimited. Smith's incredible quickness and strength let him dive for balls all over the field. His quick throws helped him fling the ball across the diamond to put out speedy runners.

Smith was a fan favorite. Sometimes he would run to his position and do a backflip before the start of the game. The Gold Glove is presented to the best defensive player at each position. Smith set a record for shortstops by winning 13 Gold Gloves. He was so good that fans called him the Wizard of Oz.

While he was strongest on defense, Smith was a quality offensive player as well. He racked up over 2,400 hits during his career. He was at his best in 1987 when he had a .303 batting average and 43 stolen bases.

## OZZIE SMITH STATS

|  |  |
|---|---|
| Batting Average | .262 |
| Hits | 2,460 |
| Home Runs | 28 |
| RBIs | 793 |

# No. 8 BARRY LARKIN

Barry Larkin played for the Cincinnati Reds for his entire career. The shortstop starred for his hometown team for 19 years. He helped lead them to a World Series title in 1990. Throughout his career, he was the face of the Reds.

Larkin was one of the best defenders in baseball. He won three Gold Gloves and had excellent defensive statistics for most of his career. He had a career fielding average that was seven points higher than the rest of the league.

Larkin's best season was in 1995 when he won the MVP Award. That year, Larkin batted .319, stole 51 bases, and won the Gold Glove. He was a 12-time All-Star. He was also the first shortstop in MLB history to have 30 home runs and 30 stolen bases in the same season.

## BARRY LARKIN STATS

|  |  |
|---|---|
| Batting Average | .295 |
| Hits | 2,340 |
| Home Runs | 198 |
| RBIs | 960 |

## No. 7 LUKE APPLING

For many years, Luke Appling was known as the greatest player in Chicago White Sox history. He didn't hit many home runs, but he was a consistently great hitter. He was known for his ability to hit the ball in any direction. He seemed to always put it in play.

Appling missed the 1944 season and most of 1945 to fight for the United States in World War II (1939–1945). If he hadn't missed those games, he may have become the eighth MLB player to reach 3,000 hits. In his best season, he led the league by hitting .388.

Many shortstops have to move to another position when they get older. Playing shortstop requires quickness and strength that some players lose as they age. Appling is one of only four players to play 100 games at shortstop when he was 40 or older. Playing for so long helped him become one of the true greats.

## LUKE APPLING STATS

| | |
|---|---|
| Batting Average | .310 |
| Hits | 2,749 |
| Home Runs | 45 |
| RBIs | 1,116 |

# No. 6 ROBIN YOUNT

Robin Yount had a 20-year career with the Milwaukee Brewers. He helped lead the team to the 1982 World Series, where they lost to the St. Louis Cardinals. Yount is regarded by many as the greatest Brewers player of all time. The team retired his jersey number in 1994. No Brewers player can wear 19 in the future.

Yount had an incredible 1982 season. He hit .331, blasted 29 home runs, and won the National League MVP. He led MLB in doubles and hits. He also won the Gold Glove. Yount's 1982 season was his best, and it's enough to make him one of the greatest of all time.

Yount went on to win another MVP award in 1989. By then, he had changed positions to center field. Still, Yount played the majority of his career at shortstop. He was elected to the Baseball Hall of Fame in 1999.

## ROBIN YOUNT STATS

| | |
|---|---|
| Batting Average | .285 |
| Hits | 3,142 |
| Home Runs | 251 |
| RBIs | 1,406 |

## No. 5 ALEX RODRIGUEZ

When Alex Rodriguez joined the Texas Rangers in 2001, he set a record for the largest contract in MLB history. The team recognized his greatness. They thought that the slugging shortstop was one of the best players the league had ever seen.

When Rodriguez was 20, he hit .358 with 36 home runs and 123 RBIs. He was second in the MVP voting that year, and his career kept getting better from there. Rodriguez was named MVP three times. He was a 14-time All-Star. He ended his career with 696 home runs and over 3,000 hits.

In 2004, Rodriguez joined the Yankees. He was suspended for the 2014 season for using steroids, or performance-enhancing drugs. That may be enough for voters to keep him out of the Hall of Fame. Still, with the way he impacted the game, no G.O.A.T. list would be complete without him.

## ALEX RODRIGUEZ STATS

|  |  |
|---|---|
| Batting Average | .295 |
| Hits | 3,115 |
| Home Runs | 696 |
| RBIs | 2,086 |

# No. 4 ERNIE BANKS

Ernie Banks was known as Mr. Cub. He played for a long time on a lot of not-so-great Chicago Cubs teams, but his play kept the fans excited even when the team was struggling. He won back-to-back MVP Awards in 1958 and 1959.

Banks was one of the first power-hitting shortstops. Before Banks, most shortstops focused on hitting for average. Banks was fast enough to field the position, but was also a very powerful hitter. He ended his career with 512 home runs. He is one of only two shortstops to hit more than 500 in their career. Banks later moved to first base after some knee injuries slowed him down.

Banks was the first Black baseball star in Chicago. He was a very important figure for racial equality in MLB. After his playing career, Banks became one of the first Black men to manage an MLB game. His jersey number was the first to be retired by the Cubs.

## ERNIE BANKS STATS

| | |
|---|---|
| Batting Average | .274 |
| Hits | 2,583 |
| Home Runs | 512 |
| RBIs | 1,636 |

## No. 3 CAL RIPKEN JR.

Cal Ripken Jr. will be remembered forever for setting a remarkable record. From June 1982 until September 1998, he did not miss a single game. Ripken's streak broke a record that was set in the 1930s by Lou Gehrig. For this record, Ripken became known as the Iron Man.

In his 21 years in the league, Ripken was an All-Star an incredible 19 times. He was very well-respected by the other players in the league. He moved to third base later in his career, but he was always known as a shortstop. In Ripken's final All-Star Game, he played third base. The game's starting shortstop, Alex Rodriguez, insisted Ripken switch positions with him to honor Ripken's career at shortstop.

Ripken won the MVP Award in 1983 and 1991. In the 1991 season, he hit .323 and had 34 home runs. It was likely the best season of his career.

## CAL RIPKEN JR. STATS

|  |  |
|---|---|
| Batting Average | .276 |
| Hits | 3,184 |
| Home Runs | 431 |
| RBIs | 1,695 |

No. 2

# DEREK JETER

Derek Jeter began playing for the New York Yankees in 1996. For almost two decades, he was the most famous player on MLB's most famous team. Jeter was known for stepping up when it counted the most. He won five World Series championships. His performances in those games earned him the nickname Captain Clutch.

Jeter's 2000 season was probably his best. The year was a special one for the Yankees and their shortstop. The Yankees won the World Series, and Jeter was the team's best player. That year, Jeter became the only player to win the All-Star Game MVP and World Series MVP in the same season.

Jeter was famous for his jump throws from shallow left field. When a ground ball was hit between the shortstop and third base positions, Jeter often grabbed the ball in the outfield grass. He would then jump in the air, twist, and throw to first base, all in one motion. Jeter's skill helped influence a whole generation of future shortstops.

## DEREK JETER STATS

| | |
|---|---|
| Batting Average | .310 |
| Hits | 3,465 |
| Home Runs | 260 |
| RBIs | 1,311 |

No. 1

# HONUS WAGNER

Honus Wagner was one of the first superstars of baseball. He started his career in the 1800s with the Louisville Colonels. But he made his biggest impact on baseball with the Pittsburgh Pirates. Wagner's exciting style of play with the Pirates helped MLB become more popular. Fans loved watching the superstar shortstop play. Without Wagner dominating the diamond, MLB may never have reached the popularity it has today.

MLB tracks a statistic called wins above replacement (WAR). It measures how much better a player is compared to a league-average player in the same position. Wagner is the all-time WAR leader among shortstops. Many argue that he is the greatest player of all time.

Wagner's power numbers are not as impressive as some other players on this list. He never hit more than 10 home runs in a season. When he played, the game was different and players hit few home runs. But Wagner often led the league in doubles, triples, and RBIs. His impact on the game and his incredible skills make Wagner the G.O.A.T.

## HONUS WAGNER STATS

| | |
|---|---|
| Batting Average | .328 |
| Hits | 3,420 |
| Home Runs | 101 |
| RBIs | 1,732 |

# EVEN MORE G.O.A.T.

There have been many other great players who played shortstop. Narrowing them down to the 10 greatest of all time is tough. Here are more players who nearly made the top-10 list.

| | |
|---|---|
| No. 11 | LOU BOUDREAU |
| No. 12 | ALAN TRAMMELL |
| No. 13 | JOE CRONIN |
| No. 14 | ARKY VAUGHN |
| No. 15 | OMAR VIZQUEL |
| No. 16 | LUIS APARICIO |
| No. 17 | NOMAR GARCIAPARRA |
| No. 18 | VERN STEPHENS |
| No. 19 | JOE SEWELL |
| No. 20 | GEORGE DAVIS |

# YOUR G.O.A.T.

It's your turn to make a G.O.A.T. list about shortstops. Start by doing research. Consider the rankings in this book. Then check out the Learn More section on page 31. Explore the books and websites to learn more about shortstops of the past and present.

You can search online for more information about great shortstops too. Check with a librarian, who may have other resources for you. You might even try reaching out to baseball teams or players to see what they think.

Once you're ready, make your list of the greatest shortstops of all time. Then ask people you know to make G.O.A.T. lists and compare them. Do you have players no one else listed? Are you missing anybody your friends think is important? Talk it over, and try to convince them that your list is the G.O.A.T.!

# GLOSSARY

**All-Star Game:** a game honoring each season's best MLB players

**batting average:** a stat found by dividing the number of times at bat into the number of base hits

**diamond:** the infield of a baseball field that forms a diamond shape

**double:** a hit that allows the batter to reach second base

**double play:** a play in which two players are put out

**fielding average:** a figure found by dividing the number of fielding chances into the number of putouts

**putout:** when a defender causes a base runner or batter to be out

**RBI:** a run in baseball that is driven in by a batter

**stolen base:** when a runner advances a base without the ball being hit

**triple:** a hit that allows the batter to reach third base

**WAR:** wins above replacement, a statistic that tracks how valuable a player is compared to an average player

## LEARN MORE

Baseball Hall of Fame
https://baseballhall.org/

Baseball: The Shortstop
https://www.ducksters.com/sports/baseball/shortstop.php

Burrell, Dean. *Baseball Biographies for Kids: The Greatest Players from the 1960s to Today.* Emeryville, CA: Rockridge Press, 2021.

Ernie Banks
https://kids.britannica.com/kids/article/Ernie-Banks/399353

Fishman, Jon M. *Baseball's G.O.A.T.: Babe Ruth, Mike Trout, and More.* Minneapolis: Lerner Publications, 2020.

Monson, James. *Behind the Scenes Baseball.* Minneapolis: Lerner Publications, 2020.

# INDEX



# PHOTO ACKNOWLEDGMENTS

Image credits: Christof Koepsel/Staff/pngimg.com, p.3; Jamie Squire/Staff/Getty Images, p.4; Keystone/Stringer/Getty Images, p.5; Ronald Martinez/Stringer/Getty Images, p.6; Rick Stewart/Stringer/Getty Images, p.7; Alamy, p.8; RLFE Pix/Alamy, p.9; John McDonough/Icon SMI/Newscom, p.10; BILL GREENBLATT/UPI/Newscom, p.11; Tom Hauck/Staff/Getty Images, p.12; Tom Hauck/Staff/Getty Images, p.13; RLFE Pix/Alamy, p.14; RLFE Pix/Alamy, p.15; Otto Greule Jr/Stringer/Getty Images, p.16; Stephen Dunn/Staff/Getty Images, p.17; Elsa/Staff/Getty Images, p.18; Al Bello/Staff/Getty Images, p.19; Alon Alexander/Alamy, p.20; Hulton Archive/Stringer/Getty Images, p.21; Ezra Shaw/Staff/Getty Images, 22; Doug Pensinger/Staff/Getty Images, p.23; Nick Laham/Staff/Getty Images, p.24; Nick Laham/Staff/Getty Images, p.25; Archive World/Alamy, p.26; Everett Collection/Newscom, p.27; Nadezhda Shpiiakina/Shutterstock, Background

Cover: Ezra Shaw/Staff/Getty Images; Matthew Stockman/Staff/Getty Images; Al Bello/Staff/Getty Images; Nadezhda Shpiiakina/Shutterstock